Survive on a Desert Island

Silver Dolphin
San Diego, California

Silver Dolphin Books
An imprint of the Advantage Publishers Group
5880 Oberlin Drive, San Diego, CA 92121-4794
www.silverdolphinbooks.com

WARNING!

This book provides useful information for difficult situations an individual may encounter, but it cannot guarantee results, nor can the publisher accept any responsibility for any injuries, damages, or loss resulting from the information within this book. The red WARNING symbol shown above denotes situations or activities that require caution. Never put yourself in danger and always seek the advice of an adult before trying any of the activities in this book, especially those highlighted with a WARNING symbol.

Created and produced by
Andromeda Children's Books
An imprint of Pinwheel Ltd.
Winchester House, 259–269 Old Marylebone Road, London NW1 5XJ United Kingdom
www.pinwheel.co.uk

Copyright © 2005 Andromeda Children's Books

ISBN 1-59223-426-7

Made in China
1 2 3 4 5 09 08 07 06 05

Author Claire Llewellyn
Managing Editor Ruth Hooper
Series Editor Deborah Murrell, **Assistant Editor** Emily Hawkins
Art Director Ali Scrivens, **Art Editor** Julia Harris, **Designer** Miranda Kennedy
Production Clive Sparling
Illustrator Peter Bull
Consultant John Marriott

Contents

Introduction

You are stranded on a desert island!
All you have with you is a backpack
with a few useful things inside.
It will be 12 days before help can arrive.

Can you survive on your own?

Can you find water and food to eat?

Can you deal with snakes and
swamps?

Can you make use of the things in
your backpack?

Here is the survival challenge!

On each page of this book, you face a different challenge.
The 12 challenges explore every aspect of life as a castaway
on a desert island—from adapting to the climate and
exploring the landscape to coping with the local plants and
animals. To meet each challenge, you need to use your wits,
the information provided, and the equipment in your
backpack. Your survival depends on using your initiative and
making the most of the natural resources around you.
Develop your survival skills and learn to face each challenge
with a resourceful and determined attitude. Once you have
escaped the island, try the quiz at the back of the book to
test your new survival skills.

What's in your backpack

garbage bag

burlap

socks

T-shirt

silky shirt

aluminum foil

wire

knife

spoon

handkerchief

plastic bags

plastic sheeting

bandanna

rope

tin can

green tea bag

walking stick

umbrella

string

whistle

cork

needle

first-aid kit

hammer

backpack

camera

Can you build a shelter?

It is your first day in an unknown environment. Building a shelter is your number-one priority. You need protection from the weather and a place to rest. Building a shelter is hard work, so you need to start working early. That way, you will complete your challenge before darkness and exhaustion set in. You must make the most of the natural resources around you to make your shelter secure and reliable.

Today's survival tools:

These things will be useful. Can you figure out how?

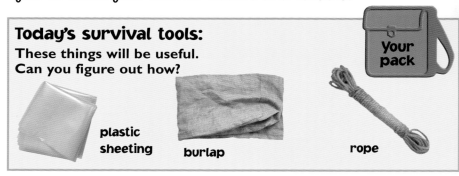

plastic sheeting

burlap

rope

Your pack

Where to camp

Q and A

Q: Is it a good idea to camp near a pond or lake?

A: No. Stagnant pond water attracts insects, some of which may bite or sting.

Q: Would a hole in the ground make a good shelter?

A: No—it will fill with water if it rains. Instead, find a place where rain will drain away.

Where is the best place to build?

Caves or overhanging rocks give protection from wind and rain, but may already be occupied by an animal. Check for signs like bones and nesting. Even a sand dune or hillside can provide some protection. Look for a dry, flat area that will not be flooded if it rains. Somewhere near trees and a stream would be ideal, so that you have fuel and water!

How do you build a simple hut?

① Make an A-frame by tying one long branch to two short ones with rope. See below for how to make natural rope.

② Wall the sides with smaller, sloping branches and cover them thickly with palm fronds or other large leaves.

③ Make your shelter waterproof by using the plastic sheeting from your backpack. If you do not have a plastic sheet, you should layer the palm fronds carefully, so that rainwater will run off. Once your shelter is complete, you can make a bed by arranging logs to form a sturdy base and driving pegs into the ground at each end to keep them from slipping. Next, make a mattress with springy branches and soft leaves, and cover it with the burlap.

Make a rope

Try it at home!

1. Choose vines or the strongest grasses you can find. Cut three long stems. Soak them in water to make them soft and flexible.

2. Tie the stems together securely at one end. Braid them evenly, as shown in the picture, and secure at the end.

This strong cord will be very useful—how many ways can you think of to use it?

How will you find water?

USE CAUTION

Now that you have built your shelter, your next priority is to find some water. Your body always needs water to function properly, and while you are living on this desert island, it is going to need lots more! But never forget that dirty water can carry diseases. You must be sure that the water you drink is absolutely pure.

Today's survival tools:

These things will be useful. Can you figure out how?

Your pack

plastic sheeting

plastic bags

sock   hammer   plastic bags

Can you collect rainwater?

The sky is gray and it looks like rain. Rain is the best and purest natural source of water, so hurry and collect some now. Grab your waterproof sheet. Spread it out and use twigs to pin the corners in place, raised off the ground so that the rain runs to the center. Place a stone or other heavy object in the middle to weigh it down. Rainwater is distilled. This means that it has evaporated into the air, leaving any impurities behind, and then cooled again. Distilled water is the safest water to drink.

Water   ○ Facts!

About 75 percent of the human body is water. You need to drink at least 8 cups per day in temperate climates and over 20 cups in hotter climates because the heat makes your body lose more water.

Is your water safe to drink?

Drinking dirty water will make you sick because it is full of bacteria. The best way to purify it is to boil the water at 212°F for at least 3 minutes. If you cannot boil it, filtering can help to purify it. Fill a sock with charcoal at the bottom, then with grass and sand, and try filtering the water through it. This will remove many of the harmful bacteria.

How can you stay hydrated?

Every drop of water you lose by breathing or sweating must be replaced by drinking. Reduce water loss by staying in the shade, keeping your skin covered, and breathing out through your nose.

5 places to look for water

Tips

1. In rivers or streams. The purest ones are those with fast-running water and stony or sandy beds.

2. Under the ground—for example, under the bed of a dry stream.

3. At the base of a cliff. Look for dripping rocks.

4. At the end of animal trails. Follow the footprints—they might lead you to water.

5. Under or near green plants, which, like us, need water to live.

What can you drink in an emergency?

What if your stored water runs out? Try looking for fruit. You may find figs, papayas, and guavas. If not, look for coconuts. Choose pale brown coconuts, which can contain up to 4 cups of refreshing milk. Pierce one of the "eyes" to drink the milk.

Papaya   Mango

A coconut contains not only milk but also protein-rich flesh. Use a hammer to crack it open.

Collect water from a plant

Try it at home!

1. Put a plastic bag over a green plant or branch and tie the open end tightly.

2. In sunlight, the leaves give off water vapor, which condenses inside the bag.

3. The water collects in a corner of the bag. Always boil water before drinking it.

Can you take the heat?

It is your third day, and the weather is scorching hot. Today's challenge is to adapt to the climate. Can you stay cool and protect yourself from the sun?

Today's survival tools:

These things will be useful. Can you figure out how?

Your pack

green tea bag

string

bandanna

The heat is exhausting. How can you keep going?

The sun and heat are making you wilt; you must change your daily routine. Get up at dawn while the air is cool—it's the best time to be active. Finish as many of your chores as possible in the morning. At midday, when the sun is hot, rest in the shade. In the late afternoon, work again until it is dark. Take advantage of cooling sea breezes by staying close to the shore. Find some large leaves that you can use to fan yourself.

5 hot tips — Tips

1. Wear loose clothing made from natural materials.

2. Rest at midday, when the sun is at its hottest.

3. Spend as much time as possible in the shade, and avoid doing too much exercise.

4. Drink plenty of fluids throughout the day.

5. Wet your clothes in cool water to help avoid overheating.

Can you protect yourself from the heat?

Aloe vera leaves

1 Skin: Do not remove your clothing; loose, light layers will protect your skin and help keep you cool. Bathing your skin with cold green tea will help prevent sunburn. If you do get burned, aloe vera juice will soothe the skin.

2 Feet: The sand is much too hot to walk on, so keep your shoes on all the time. If they tear, repair them with string.

3 Eyes: Your eyes are sore from the dazzling light: you need to find a way to protect them. Without sunglasses, it is hard to work in the bright sun. By making thin slits in a piece of tree bark and attaching natural string to each side, you can make your own sunglasses and beat the glare.

4 Head: Keep the sun off your head with a bandanna, and wet it whenever you can. Try adding a brim to the bandanna, using a piece of bark from one of the trees around you.

What if you have heatstroke?

Heatstroke occurs when the body is so hot that it can no longer regulate temperature. Symptoms include headaches, lack of sweating, and dizziness. If you have any of these, drench your clothing in water, lie in the shade, and sip water slowly throughout the day. Heatstroke victims have a temperature above 104°F, but it is difficult to check your temperature without a thermometer. Try cooling your hand in water and placing the back of your hand on your forehead. If it feels hot and very clammy, try to cool down as soon as you can.

Make a sundial

Try it at home!

1. Push a tall stick into the ground.

2. Mark the end of the stick's shadow when the sun rises in the morning, and again in the evening just before it sets.

3. Draw a semicircle around the stick that connects the first and last points, and mark the midpoint (midday). You now have a "dial" on which to keep track of time.

Will you find food?

USE CAUTION

Food is running low, so you will need to find some more in the wild. You are surrounded by plants and animals, but which of them are good and safe to eat? Searching for food takes a lot of effort. This is no time to be squeamish!

Today's survival tools:

Your pack

These things will be useful. Can you figure out how?

knife   spoon

Where should you look?

As you get to know the island, you will soon learn where to find food. There may be coconuts, seaweed, and shellfish on the shore, and fruit and nuts inland. You may be able to dig up sweet potatoes with your spoon. If food is scarce, you will need to overcome your natural instinct to avoid certain things; in survival situations, people have resorted to eating just about anything!

Can any food be stored?

Searching for food takes time and energy, so foods you can store are a real bonus. Dried seaweed can later be ground up and boiled to make nutritious soup. Look for it in shallow water. Only choose healthy seaweed that is still attached to rocks. Wash it to get rid of tiny creatures and sand, then hang it up to dry for a few days.

Food tips

Tips

1. Don't gather rotting or overripe food.

2. Don't overpick from good plants— allow them to grow back.

3. Don't eat anything you are not sure about. Leave all fungi alone.

4. You'll find shellfish in shallow streams as well as the ocean.

5. If you pick seaweed, don't destroy it; leave plenty attached to the rock.

Animals to eat

There are not a lot of poisonous animals, so meat can be a safer form of food. Poorly prepared meat, however, can cause serious illness. Always wash and cook food well to remove bacteria, parasites, and impurities. Remove wings and legs from all insects before cooking. Open shellfish with a blunt knife to avoid injury.

Plants to eat

Some tropical plants are highly nutritious. Others must be avoided, as they can contain poisons. Never eat anything unless you are sure it is safe—knowing what is safe can save your life. You can test plants for edibility by rubbing them on a sensitive area of skin, such as the inner wrist, to see if a reaction occurs.

Safe animals

- **All birds**
- **Nonstinging insects, including ants, grubs, and beetles**
- **Worms: dig them up with a shovel or spoon and drop them into water, where they will clean themselves**
- **Crayfish: found beneath rocks in streams**
- **Shrimp, crabs, and lobsters: catch at night on the shore**
- **Mollusks: boil in the shell and pry open with a blunt knife**

Safe plants

- **Papayas**
- **Coconuts**
- **Bananas**
- **Mangoes**
- **Sugarcane**
- **Cashew nuts**
- **Pineapples**
- **Palms**

Unsafe plants

- **Mushrooms**
- **Overripe fruit**
- **Beans, bulbs, or seeds from pods**
- **Plants with a three-leaved growth pattern**
- **Grain heads with pink, purple, or black spurs**

Unsafe animals

- **Biting or stinging insects**
- **Hairy or brightly colored insects**
- **Spiders, mosquitoes, and ticks**
- **Mollusks that are not covered by water at high tide**
- **Brightly colored frogs**
- **Any animals that you find dead**
- **Fish with poisonous skin**

Protein

Facts!

Beef contains 20 percent protein, whereas insects are up to 80 percent protein. This fact makes bugs, beetles, grubs, and larvae an important source of protein in survival situations.

How will you catch fish?

Now that you are eating wild food, it is time to try to catch a fish. Can you make a net or a hook and line? Can you discover where and when fish like to feed? How patient and determined are you? This challenge could be tricky!

Today's survival tools:

Your pack

These things will be useful. Can you figure out how?

T-shirt   string

When and where should you fish?

Fish are found in freshwater rivers as well as the salty ocean. When it is cool, they swim in sunny water. When it is hot, they move to deeper, cooler water or seek shade under a bank. You need to cast your line at a time of day when the fish are feeding. This is usually in the early morning, late afternoon, or evening. A good place to fish is where water is forced through a narrow gap or gushes over rocks.

Eating fish

Facts!

- Avoid fish that have spines, horns, or an unusual shape, as they might be poisonous.
- Never eat dead fish you have not caught yourself.
- It is safe to eat raw saltwater fish as long as it is very fresh.

How can you catch a fish?

There are several techniques to practice:

1. Make a fishing line with a branch and string.
2. Use a long, sharpened stick as a spear.
3. Try using your bare hands!

Can fish be stored?

Fish can be preserved in the sun. Remove their heads, tails, and fins, cut them open and take out their insides and bones, then wash them thoroughly. Hang them in strong sunshine until the flesh feels brittle. You can use them later to make soup.

What should you use as bait?

It is best to tempt fish with their normal diet—live maggots, worms, insects, shellfish, shrimp, and tiny fish. Do not be squeamish about using live bait; its movement will attract the fish.

Fishing tips

Tips

1. Fish often feed before a storm, so if you feel the weather changing, it is a good time to catch your food.

2. If there is a heavy current, fish will rest in calmer places around rocks and dunes.

3. There are no poisonous freshwater fish, so if you find a stream, you know you are safe.

4. You must cook freshwater fish to remove parasites.

5. Some fish feed at night, so leave lines out overnight to catch them while you sleep.

Nutrition

Facts!

Fish are an excellent source of protein, vitamins, and minerals. Oily fish contain vitamin A, which helps your vision in dim light, and vitamin D, which is needed for healthy bones.

Make a fishing net

Try it at home!

1. To make your net, find a forked twig. Thread the forks through the hem of an old T-shirt, through two tiny holes.

2. When the ends meet, push them out through a hole and tie them together with string. Tie off the armholes and neck hole to make the base of the net secure.

What do you know about fire?

Fire has many uses in addition to cooking. It can be used to keep you and your clothes dry and warm, to keep insects away, and to signal for help. Making a fire is dangerous but is a vital survival skill.

USE CAUTION

WARNING

It is useful to know how to build a fire, but you should never try to make a fire on your own. Always have adult supervision. When learning how to build a fire, you should remember these important things.

What should be used as fuel?

Tinder is something that will catch fire easily, so you can use it to start a fire. Dry grass, fluffy seeds, and even cotton balls make really good tinder. To get the fire burning, you will need kindling, like long, fine twigs or dried seaweed. To keep a campfire going, you will need to find wood—preferably driftwood on the beach or dead wood that has not fallen onto damp ground. Standing trees, dead or alive, are home to birds and insects, so leave them intact.

Use small pieces of wood—no larger than the diameter of an adult wrist—that can be broken with your hands. This practice avoids having to use a saw or hatchet (which you probably won't have handy on a desert island!) and the wood will readily burn to ash.

Where is a good spot for a fire?

You should find an area away from your shelter where wood is plentiful. Stay away from anything that can catch fire accidentally, like bushes or undergrowth, and keep wood and other sources of fuel away from the fire. Fires should be built on sand or soil and you should have water, sand, or loose dirt at hand, ready to put out the fire. Never leave a fire unattended and be sure to thoroughly extinguish all fires: when you're ready to stop using the fire, stop adding new wood and instead toss in burned ends of wood. Allow the wood to burn to white ash, thoroughly soak with water, and cover it with sand and dirt.

Fire

Q: Where is the best place to find firewood?

A: Look for dry, dead wood caught in the branches of trees.

Q: What if it is too windy to light a fire?

A: Make your campfire in a sheltered area, or dig a shallow trench.

Q: Is a bigger campfire always better?

A: No—big fires need a lot of fuel and their heat is often wasted.

WARNING

USE CAUTION

Never try to make a fire on your own. Always have adult supervision.

Will you explore the island?

You now have a shelter, water, and food. Your new challenge is to explore the island. This will require planning. What kind of terrain will you cross? Can you find your way around the island? Can you find your way back? Surveying your environment and becoming an expert in simple navigation could save your life.

Why should you explore?

Although you feel at home in your immediate surroundings, think of what would happen if a fire struck or a dangerous predator arrived. If you have to leave quickly, it helps to know the lay of the land.

What are the risks?

Traveling exposes you to many risks. You could get lost or run out of water; in the woods you might be attacked by insects; on the beach you could be cut off by the tide; in the hills you might be caught in a low cloud, and so on. Before you set out, make a plan. Use binoculars to examine the land and decide on the best route. If you have no binoculars, find a high vantage point and survey the area to note any likely dangers.

Today's survival tools:

your pack

These things will be useful. Can you figure out how?

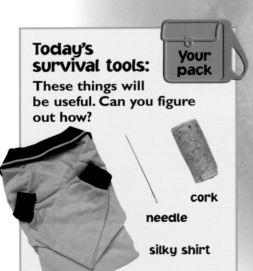

cork

needle

silky shirt

Walk for one hour: 🔖 Facts!

- On flat terrain, with a light load: 3 miles

- On hilly terrain, carrying a heavy load: 1.5 miles

- On a moonless night, with a heavy load: 0.5 miles

- In a thick forest: 0.25 miles

What is the best time to explore?

Do not travel in the heat of the day; either set out at dawn or wait until evening. If the moon is bright, it may be best to travel at night, when it is cool. If you travel along a beach, be sure to start after high tide so that you can reach higher ground before the tide returns.

Which direction should you take?

Without a compass, it can be difficult to tell which direction to take. You can make a compass using just a cork and needle. Stroke the needle across silky fabric 20 times in the same direction. This will magnetize the needle. Float the cork in water and place the needle on top. It will swing around to point north/south.

Exploring Tips

1. Carry plenty of water with you.

2. Don't hurry. Try to walk at a steady pace.

3. Don't overheat. Open your clothing if you feel too warm.

4. Take regular rest breaks—about 10 minutes every hour.

5. Decide on your direction and maintain it by choosing a prominent landmark in the distance and heading toward it.

6. Avoid thick vegetation— you may encounter thorny plants. If you do get snared, do not panic, but back out slowly.

How to draw a map

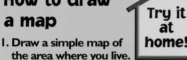

Try it at home!

1. Draw a simple map of the area where you live.

2. Mark all the landmarks that help you to find your way around.

3. Make a grid, as shown here, to help you locate different places using a reference. For example, the school is in square 2B. This is a coordinate.

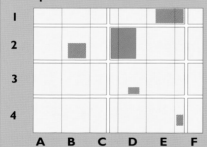

How do you get around?

If possible, follow any existing tracks—this will be much easier than hacking through dense bushes. Riverbanks are clearly defined routes. Follow them if you want to reach the ocean or inland lakes. You can also leave stones in piles or arranged in arrow shapes. This way, you'll be able to find your way back.

Can you handle hazards?

Your desert island may look idyllic, but at times you will encounter natural hazards. Could you cross a river, get out of quicksand, or escape from a flood or fire? Today you are faced with challenges that directly threaten your survival. How will you cope?

Today's survival tools:
**These things will be useful.
Can you figure out how?**

Your pack

walking stick

handkerchief

Hazards

Tips

1. Be careful to never start a brush fire. When you put out a campfire, spread and wet the embers, then cover them with sand and dirt.

2. Always walk with a strong stick. It can be used to test the ground, help you cross water, and support your weight.

3. Never cross a stream in the dark, or if the other side is not visible.

4. In a flood, your drinking water may become contaminated. If you are unsure, always boil water again before drinking it.

Fire!

In hot, dry, windy weather, there could be brush or forest fires. Be alert to the smell of smoke, or animals acting nervously. If the wind is blowing toward the fire, move into the wind. If the wind is behind the fire, the flames will blow toward you very fast! Look for a stream or a clearing in the trees where there would be little fuel for the fire. Lie down, breathe close to the ground, and stay there until the fire has passed. If you can, wet your clothing and put a jacket over your head. Cover your mouth with a handkerchief so that you don't breathe in too much smoke.

Rapids!

If a river blocks your path and there are no natural bridges, you must brave the water. Look for a good crossing point—a place where the riverbed is firm and the water is fairly shallow. Beware of rocks, strong currents, and steep banks. Keep your shoes on and cross over slowly, using a strong walking stick for support. If the current is fast or if you have to cross near rapids, use a strong rope to make a safety belt. Tie one end to your waist and make a loop at the other end. Throw the loop to the opposite bank and anchor it around a secure branch or rock, then pull yourself to safety across the river.

Crossing a river safely, using a rope to anchor you to the opposite side

Quicksand!

You are walking near the beach when you find yourself sinking. It's quicksand! Try to stay calm and move slowly. Head toward firm ground and try to grab some long grass. If you are stuck, drop everything but your stick and lie back, spreading out your arms and legs. Place your stick crosswise beneath your hips to help support you. Spreading your body weight over a large area helps keep you from sinking. Once you are floating, drag yourself to firmer ground.

Floating on quicksand

Flood!

After days of heavy rain, rivers and streams may flood. If so, try to be prepared. Find a safe route to a vantage point on high ground and move all your belongings there. If water levels continue to rise and you find yourself caught in a flood, grab hold of a log or anything that floats past, and make your way slowly to safety.

What if animals attack you?

DAY 9

You faced natural hazards yesterday; new dangers lie ahead today. There are animals on your desert island and in the surrounding ocean. Some of these animals are predators. If they attacked you, what would you do? Would you be able to overcome your fear? Could you escape and survive?

Today's survival tools:

Your pack

These things will be useful. Can you figure out how?

bandanna

umbrella

Crocodiles and alligators!

These two animals are related and look alike. If you meet one of these large reptiles, slowly back away. If it comes toward you, use your umbrella to hit it on the nose or in the eyes. If it bites you, punch its snout hard to make it open its mouth. Holding a bandanna over its eyes may calm it down.

Crocodiles

Facts!

- Crocodiles are found near swamps, rivers, and tidal pools.
- Never enter the water at dusk.
- Never approach a crocodile's nest, eggs, or young.

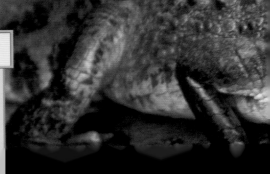

Snakes ○ Facts!

- Snakes are found in trees and in water, as well as on the ground.
- Never climb trees or move rocks or logs with your bare hands.
- Never swim in muddy rivers.

Snakes!

If you see a snake, back away slowly, giving it a lot of room. Snakes can strike half their body length away, and some are over 6 feet long! A loud display will often frighten a snake. Try flapping your umbrella up and down to scare the snake away.

Ants!

Fire ants and driver ants give painful stings. Millions of the ants form long columns and kill everything in their path. If you see a column, get out of its way. If you walk into a column, try to keep still. The ants are following a scent trail, and if you break it, they will attack you. If this happens, run away. Jump into water if you can, but only if it is safe to do so.

Ants ○ Facts!

- Most ants are found in woodland, where there are materials to build their nests.
- Learn to recognize an ants' nest.
- Never disturb a nest.

Sharks!

You are swimming in the ocean when you see a shark! Try not to panic—sharks rarely attack people. Do not shout, splash, or kick. Get out of the water as quickly as you can by swimming quietly, using the breaststroke. If the shark attacks, punch it in the gills or between the eyes.

Sharks ○ Facts!

- Sharks are attracted by blood, fish, and bait. They are most active in the evening.
- Never swim after dusk.
- Never enter the water with an open wound.
- Never swim where you fish.

Could you cope in a storm?

Today, a storm is on the way: the sky is black, the wind is strong, and you can hear thunder in the distance. It is vital that you prepare for the storm. Can you find shelter from the wind and rain, and avoid being struck by lightning?

Today's survival tools:
These things will be useful. Can you figure out how?

Your pack

rope

garbage bag

How can you prepare for the storm?

Watch for weather indicators so that you don't get caught in a storm. For example, pinecones open their scales when the air is dry and close them before it rains. If a storm is brewing, you must move quickly. Leave the shore and move inland, onto higher ground. Storms can last as long as 72 hours, so take water, food, and fuel.

> **Facts!**

How far away is the storm?

Count the seconds between a flash of lightning and the rumble of thunder. Divide this number by five to calculate the distance in miles. Which do you think travels faster, light or sound?

Where is the best place to shelter?

The best place to shelter from a storm is a dry cave in a hillside or cliff, with no risk of flooding. Build a fire at the back of the cave—the smoke will rise and drift out. If you are caught outside, keep dry in a poncho (see activity box on next page).

Can you avoid being struck by lightning?

Lightning happens when negative charges at the bottom of the clouds are attracted to positive charges in the ground, causing dazzling sparks of electricity to jump between them. How can you keep out of harm's way? Lightning usually strikes the highest places, so stay away from hilltops and wide-open spaces, and do not shelter under trees. Metal conducts electricity, so put away any metal objects. If you can, stay dry and safe deep inside a cave until the storm has passed.

Storm dos and don'ts

Tips

1. **Do** keep away from the coast, where the storm's effects will be greater.

2. **Don't** shelter near the front of a cave—lightning can spark across the gap.

3. **Do** use a coil of rope to sit on—it is a good insulator for protection from lightning.

4. **Don't** shelter under a single tree—lightning is likely to strike the tree.

5. **Do** avoid being near anything that might fall on you, like small trees.

Mosquitoes

Facts!

Rain encourages mosquitoes to hatch. They carry diseases and can give you a nasty bite. Cover exposed skin and keep a campfire smoking at night to drive them away. Make a natural insect repellent with crushed lemon-scented plants.

What happens in the eye of a storm?

If the weather suddenly calms, do not relax just yet—you could be in the eye of the storm. This is an area of calm, with light winds and no rain. Stay sheltered and prepare for the other side of the storm to reach you. Do not return to your hut until you are certain it is safe to do so.

Make a waterproof poncho

Take a plastic garbage bag and cut both sides to open it out flat.

Try it at home!

1. Fold the bag in half and cut an 8-inch semicircle in the center. When opened flat, you will have a circle.

2. Place your head through the hole. The poncho will sit on your shoulders and rain will run off.

Could you treat an injury?

It is hard to avoid accidents when you are living in the wild. Yet medical help is a long way away. What would you do if you hurt yourself? First aid is a vital skill that might help you survive.

Today's survival tools:

These things will be useful. Can you figure out how?

Your pack

first-aid kit with safety pins, dressing pads, and bandages

bandanna

How will you react in an emergency?

In any emergency, it is important to remain calm. Panic wastes time and keeps you from thinking clearly. Being prepared and knowing what to do will help you to act sensibly and quickly.

4 signs of a broken bone

 Tips

1. Swelling or bruising
2. A bent appearance
3. Bone sticking out through skin
4. Severe pain

How do you treat a broken bone?

If you break a bone, you will naturally hold it in the most comfortable position you can. Find a piece of wood or a stick that you can use as a splint. Tie it securely, but not too tightly, onto the injured area so that it supports both above and below the broken bone. For how to tie a sling, see page 27.

How to tie a sling

Try it at home!

1. Take a large triangular cloth or bandanna and slide it under the armpit of your "broken" arm.

2. Bring one corner around the back of your neck. Bring the other corner up to meet it.

3. Tie the two corners together.

4. Pin the third corner in place.

How do you treat a bleeding wound?

1. Press the edges of the wound together—in time, it will begin to seal.

2. Press hard with a pad until the bleeding stops.

3. Hold the wounded area as high as you can. Gravity will help to ease the blood flow.

4. Now put a clean pad on the wound and bandage it firmly to hold it in place. Change the pad daily to avoid infection.

How do you treat an animal bite?

1. Wash the wound thoroughly for about five minutes to get rid of germs.

2. Dry it gently and cover with a bandage.

3. Change the bandage daily to keep the wound clean. If you are bitten by a snake, don't try to suck out the poison—this can cause the poison to enter your body through your mouth.

Can you get off the island?

Congratulations! You have survived for 11 days on a desert island, and have just one last challenge to perform. A plane is flying over the island today. Can you somehow attract the pilot's attention? Can you get him or her to rescue you? Do not waste this opportunity—it may be your one and only chance of escape!

Today's survival tools:
These things will be useful. Can you figure out how?

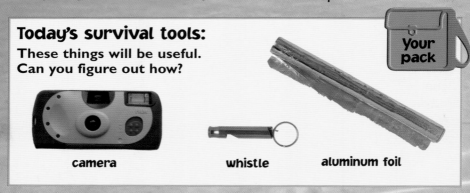

Your pack

camera   whistle   aluminum foil

What is the best way to attract attention?

When pilots are flying over land, they notice anything out of the ordinary. Good, clear signals will attract their attention. Find the highest, flattest area from which to signal. Now, decide what kind of signal is best for the time, the place, and the weather. In daylight, you could make a smoky fire. At night, you will do better with a bright fire.

Distress signal   Facts!

The international distress signal is "SOS" (Save Our Souls). This can be transmitted in Morse code by using three short signals, three long signals, and three short signals (...---...).

28

Can you send a smoke signal?

A fire is easily seen from the air; in fact, three fires in a triangle is an internationally recognized distress signal. Have three fires prepared and ready for lighting at the first sign of possible help. Throw green (not dry) plants on top of the fire to make a lot of smoke.

How can you signal on a sunny day?

On a clear day, the best way to send a signal is to reflect the sun's rays. Smooth, shiny things make the best reflectors. If you do not have a mirror, aluminum foil will do. Tilt your reflector in the direction of the sun until a flash is reflected on the ground, then move the flash up toward the plane. If the sun has set by the time the plane arrives, your reflector will not work. After dark, use your camera flash to send a signal.

Rescue

Q and A

Q: Are you sure a flash will be seen?

A: In good conditions, a flash can be seen for many miles.

Q: How can I tell whether the pilot has seen my message?

A: The pilot will tilt the plane's wings or flash green signal lights.

Q: The rescue plane has landed a long way away. How can the pilot find me?

A: Give six short blasts on your whistle, pause, then repeat.

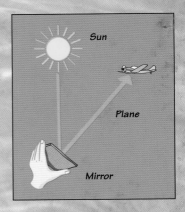

Sun

Plane

Mirror

So you think you could survive?

How much have you learned about survival in the wild? Can you answer these questions correctly? All the information can be found in the book. After taking the quiz, check your answers on page 32.

1. **Where is the best place to build a shelter?**

a. In a hollow in the ground

b. On top of a hill

c. On dry, flat ground, near trees and water

2. **What should you do if you are short of water?**

a. Eat juicy fruit

b. Eat seaweed

c. Drink seawater

3. **You are very hot. To cool down, you should:**

a. Take off your clothes

b. Rest in the shade

c. Have a hot drink

4. **Which of these things is safe to eat?**

a. Mushrooms

b. Stinging insects

c. Worms

5. **What is one of the best times to catch fish?**

a. Midday

b. Dusk

c. Low tide

6. **Which of these would you use to start a campfire?**

a. Dry grass

b. Dead logs

c. Dried fish

7. **You see pinecones with their scales wide open. This means it will be:**

a. Wet

b. Windy

c. Dry

8. **What can help you find a north/south direction?**

a. A magnetized needle

b. A dead tree

c. The tides

9. **What should you avoid when crossing a river?**

a. A firm riverbed

b. Steep banks

c. Stepping-stones

10. **You've seen a crocodile. What should you do?**

a. Keep still, then slowly back away

b. Shout at it and wave your arms

c. Throw it a fish

11. **What would you do if an alligator attacked?**

a. Run away fast

b. Hit it on the nose

c. Shout for help

12. **You're bleeding badly. What would be a good way to treat the wound?**

a. Wash the wound in the sea

b. Pour tea on the wound

c. Press the two edges of the wound together

13. **What does "SOS" stand for?**

a. Save Our Souls

b. Sharks On the Sea

c. Sticks Or Stones

14. **Which of these is the best signal to use at night?**

a. A reflector

b. A ground-to-air message

c. A bright fire

Now check your answers with those on page 32. How many did you answer correctly?

12–14 correct answers:

Congratulations; you're a true survivor!

9–11 correct answers:

Pretty good; you'd probably make it through!

4–8 correct answers:

You might be lucky and survive, but you could probably do with learning some more skills!

1– 3 correct answers:

Try not to get stranded on a desert island—or brush up on your survival skills first!

Index

Picture credits: All images supplied by Corbis. 1, 4–5, 20–21, 28–29, 30–31 Craig Tuttle; 2–3 Casa Productions; 6–7 Ivor Fulcher; 8–9 Sergio Pitamitz; 10–11 Jeff Turnau; 12–13 Bernardo Bucci; 14–15 Ralph A. Clevenger; 16–17 Doug Wilson; 18–19 Danny Lehman; 22–23 Ron Sanford; 26–27 Joe McDonald; 28–29 Neil Robinowitz.

Answers to quiz on pages 30–31:

1. c, *2.* a, *3.* b, *4.* c, *5.* b, *6.* a, *7.* c, *8.* a, *9.* b, *10.* a, *11.* b, *12.* c, *13.* a, *14.* c.